Closing Circles

50 Activities for Ending the Day in a Positive Way

K–6

Dana Januszka • Kristen Vincent

Responsive Classroom®

Center for Responsive Schools, Inc.

All net proceeds from the sale of this book support the work of Center for Responsive Schools, Inc., a not-for-profit educational organization and the developer of the *Responsive Classroom*® approach to teaching.

ISBN 978-1-892989-52-9
Library of Congress Control Number: 2012936532

Thanks to the children whose drawings grace these pages.

Cover and book design by Helen Merena
Cover photograph © Alice Proujansky. All rights reserved.

Center for Responsive Schools, Inc.
85 Avenue A, P.O. Box 718
Turners Falls, MA 01376-0718

800-360-6332
www.responsiveclassroom.org

Fifth printing 2017

Printed on recycled paper

*To our beautiful daughters, who remind us
each day to enjoy every moment, and to always
end the day with a smile.*

What Is a Closing Circle?

It used to be that at 3:30 every afternoon, our class-rooms would erupt into chaos. Children chatted away; backpacks were strewn in one direction, lunchboxes in another; notices and class work were scattered over the floor.

As teachers, we were incredibly frustrated. During the day, we put so much thought into building a positive learning environment from arrival time to group discussion to individual work. We even took steps to make sure lunch and recess were peaceful learning times for the children.

But at the end of the day it all fell apart. The students, and we ourselves, would end up leaving school feeling frazzled, as though nothing had been tied up before everyone ran out the door.

Things began to change when we learned about closing circles. Here was a strategy that allowed us to end the day with structure, sanity, and a strong sense of community.

Now, at the end of the day, we guide students in packing up and doing their classroom jobs. Then, with their backpacks on or placed behind them, the children gather in a circle on the rug. Going around the circle, each student says something about some activity or learning from the day, or the group plays a quick game.

Simple, but as we say good-bye to each student at the door, we feel calmer and more energized, and we can tell that the children feel the same.

* * *

A closing circle is a strategy for bringing a peaceful end to the school day. It doesn't take very long—students gather for five to ten minutes to do a brief activity or two and then go on to dismissal—but it has a big impact on students' learning and behavior and the classroom climate.

Many teachers begin the day with a morning meeting to set a tone of community and engaged learning and to launch students into the day's work with pleasant anticipation.

A five- to ten-minute closing circle wraps up the day on a similarly positive note. Whether students had a good day or a tough day, a closing circle can help build trust and cooperation in the classroom. This safe environment enables students to take risks so that they can do their best learning.

Wrapping up the day this way benefits the teacher, too. A hectic dismissal can leave teachers feeling exhausted and unproductive, even if the majority of the day went smoothly. After using closing circles, many teachers report more positive energy and attitudes not only in their students, but in themselves as well.

In short, closing circles can help students learn better and teachers teach better. It's a small investment of time that makes a big difference in the life of the classroom.

In this book, we offer fifty tried and true closing circle activities. But first, some basics about this strategy.

What Do Children Do in a Closing Circle?

What takes place during the few minutes of a closing circle can vary from class to class and from day to day. Here are just a few things a class might do:

- Sing a song together
- Think about an accomplishment from their day
- Set a personal goal for the following day
- Play a game
- Send a friendly good-bye around the circle

The choice depends on the children's developmental abilities, your personal style, and, importantly, the kind of day the class had (see "Choose Activities Purposefully" on page 6 for more).

The common thread that runs through these activities is their focus on the positive. A closing circle is not the time to address problems going on in the class or to make class decisions. Those tasks can wait until the next day. Rather, it's a time to wrap up the day in a way that leaves students feeling calm, competent, and upbeat about their learning.

(If the class has a problem that needs solving, use a collaborative problem-solving strategy at a time of day other than the closing circle. To learn about such strategies, see *Solving Thorny Behavior Problems: How Teachers and Students Can Work Together* by Caltha Crowe, 2009, or free articles on this topic, all available at www.responsiveclassroom.org.)

The Benefits of Closing Circles: A Closer Look

How exactly do closing circles help build a positive classroom environment?

They allow children to celebrate accomplishments.

Many things, large and small, are worth celebrating over the course of a school day. Learning a new skill, completing a challenging assignment, practicing a fire drill in record time, and showing kindness to a classmate are just a few examples. Pausing to note these important day-to-day accomplishments helps cultivate a positive classroom environment. But with all the demands teachers face each day, we often feel that we don't have the time. Setting aside a few minutes at the end of each day ensures that these happenings don't go unnoticed.

They give children a chance to reflect on learning.

As many educators know, children can deepen their under-standing and stretch their thinking skills when we lead them to think back on information they took in, question its validity, make connections, draw conclusions, or plan for next steps. It's hard in today's fast-paced, jam-packed class-rooms to always have time for this kind of reflection unless we deliberately plan for it. Building in time for reflection during a closing circle is one way to ensure that this happens.

They help children gain a sense of belonging.

To take the risks necessary for learning, children need to feel a sense of belonging and significance. Knowing this, many teachers strive to create that powerful atmosphere of com-munity in the classroom. At the close of the day, singing a song together, playing a math review game, or sharing how the class overcame an obstacle are just a few ways that this sense of community can be strengthened.

Choose Activities Purposefully

When choosing or adapting ideas for your class, keep these things in mind:

Consider what kind of day the class had.

- Was it a smooth day? A rocky day?
- What academic or social skills did the class especially focus on?
- What content are the students studying right now?

Like any classroom activity, closing circle activities will benefit students the most when you use them purposefully—to reinforce skills they're working on, to give them a lift when their energy is flagging, to help restore community when needed, or to meet other goals.

For example, if the class worked hard on a math skill, they might celebrate their effort with a class cheer such as "Give This Group a Hand" (page 50). Or they might do an activity that reinforces the math skill, such as "Did You Know?" (page 44).

If the day was particularly challenging, you might choose an activity that helps children focus on envisioning a positive start to the next day (for example, "Make a Wish," page 90).

Think about students' skills and capabilities.

Each activity in this book is labeled with a suggested grade range. Consider these labels as you choose activities. Keep in mind, however, that the labels provide just a general guide and that every class is unique. Observe your class and consider where they are in their development. And don't be afraid to look outside your grade range for ideas—some activities labeled for other grades could work well for your particular class. Certainly if you teach second or third graders, be sure to check out the activities in both the K–2 and 3–6 ranges.

Also remember that you can adjust virtually any activity to make it appropriate for your students' needs. Often by simply changing the questions you pose or modifying one step, you can decrease or increase an activity's level of sophistication.

Finally, you'll see many activities labeled K–6. These are likely to work as written for all elementary grades. But even with these broadly useful activities, you may want to adjust a detail or two to fit your class's needs.

Make each activity your own.

When using any of the activities in this book, don't feel tied to the exact movements or tune. If you don't know the tune of a song, just chant the words to a beat. Honor student contributions and create special variations that are unique to your class. The important thing is that you make each activity meaningful for the students you're teaching.

Choose short activities when time is tight.

Rushing through an activity usually means losing its effectiveness. So on especially busy days, try to do end-of-day tasks earlier in the day and choose short activities for the closing circle. For example, if on certain days the class doesn't return from a special until five minutes before the end of the day, you might have the children pack up before they go to the special and then do just a simple group good-bye or group cheer (such as "Circle of Hands," page 38) when they gather for the closing circle during those last five minutes. Even a quick reflection or celebration can provide a meaningful closure to the day.

Don't be afraid to repeat activities.

Children, especially in the younger grades, often enjoy doing the same activities over and over, so coming back to old favorites time and again can be very effective.

More Keys to Successful Closing Circles

Protect those five to ten minutes.

You don't need a lot of time to have an effective closing circle: five to ten minutes should do it. But you do need to protect this time from intrusions. Otherwise, the gathering will feel rushed rather than calm and uplifting.

It's true that in today's classrooms, carving out five to ten minutes can be challenging. But with some planning, end-of-day routines will be efficient, clearing out enough uninterrupted closure time. For ideas, see "Seven Ways to Find 5–10 Minutes" on page 13.

Make sure everyone takes part.

For a sense of community, every student and adult in the room should participate in closing circles. This is not a time for children to finish assignments or to complete end-of-day jobs.

Teach closing circle routines.

As with any classroom proce-dure, closing circle expecta-tions and routines need to be carefully taught if children are to do them successfully. Here are the closing circle skills that students most commonly need to be taught. (Even if you've taught similar skills for morning meetings or other activities, it will be helpful to reteach or review them for use in closing circles.)

A Simple Way to Teach Routines

For many of the closing circle routines listed here, children will need to see the routine modeled and then practice it under your guidance. Inter-active Modeling, a strategy of the *Responsive Classroom*® approach to education, is a quick and effective way to do this teaching.

To learn more about Interactive Modeling, see page 18.

- **How to know it's time for the closing circle.** Is it when you ring the chime or when a bell rings over the loudspeaker? Is it whenever students complete their end-of-day jobs? Whatever the signal, teach and practice it with students.

- **What to do with belongings.** Children usually pay better attention if their hands are empty and their belongings out of sight. So teach them where to park

9

A Final Good-bye

As students leave the room, stand at the door and say good-bye to each of them. Some teachers give each child a high five or a peace sign, or do the class's secret handshake. This personal touch takes so little time yet adds so much to each child's feeling valued.

backpacks and papers before coming to the closing circle. If students need to have their belongings nearby, teach them how to put those things behind their bodies, outside of the circle.

- **How to form a circle.** Have a dedicated space large enough for everyone to sit together in a circle. Then teach how to form the circle efficiently. Some teachers, especially of younger grades, assign seats in the circle. Some have students sit alphabetically or by dismissal routine (walkers together, bus riders together, etc.). Others let students choose their seats. Whatever your method, make sure everyone understands and knows how to use it.

- **How to respond to signals.** How will you signal during a closing circle that it's time for the student who's speaking to give someone else a turn or that you need everyone's quiet attention? Some teachers use a chime, a rain stick, or a raised hand as the signal. Choose something that will work consistently in your classroom, decide how children should respond (for example, quickly wrap up their conversation, get quiet, and look at you), and teach them these expectations.

- **What the general rules are for any activities you do.** Think about rules for who goes first and last, who is next, and so forth. Teach these before they come into play in closing circle activities.

10

- How to transition from the circle to line-up. You might call out categories ("Anyone wearing purple may line up" or "Anyone who likes strawberry ice cream may line up"). Or you might play a game such as Pop-Up Number (children count around the circle to a designated number—for example, three; each child who says "three" pops up and gets in line). Also decide where students should line up and what standing in line in a safe and friendly way looks and sounds like. Then teach these routines to students.

Carefully choose the open-ended questions you ask.

Many of the activities in this book have the teacher posing an open-ended question about the day for the children to answer, either out loud or privately. In either case, make sure your questions are meaningful to the children by thinking about their interests and the academic and social skills they're working on.

Be careful to avoid questions that could cause or fuel social problems among the children. For example, in a sixth grade class that's struggling with cliques, asking the children to rate how the class as a whole is doing in this area could be divisive. A more effective approach might be to ask the children how they personally did on a concrete act of inclusiveness. For example, "How did you do on saying good morning to a large number of classmates during arrival time today?"

Anticipate a variety of responses to questions.

Think ahead about the types of responses students may give when you prompt reflection or recall of facts. In particular, be prepared for two common situations that can sometimes be challenging:

- **Students respond that something went poorly for them that day.** If an individual student responds this way, follow up with her privately to see if you can help. If it seems that something is a concern for many students, acknowledge this concern by summarizing what you heard. For example, "I notice that many of you are not feeling good about recess today." Then set a new, positive goal for the class or state how you'll follow up with them. "Let's set aside some time tomorrow before recess to figure out what's going on so you can have more fun together."

- **A student gives an incorrect answer to a factual question.** Give the student another chance to answer (ask if he'd like a clue from you or other students), or open up the question to the class. Remember that the goal is to keep closing circles cooperative and enable students to leave school feeling encouraged and competent.

12

Seven Ways to Find 5–10 Minutes

Right about now, you may be thinking, "Closing circles sound great. But with everything going on each day, how do I find the time?"

The key is efficiency. If you manage the end of the day efficiently, you can find a surprising amount of time. Here are seven ideas. Choose the ones that might best help you and the particular group of students you're teaching right now. The goal: get packing up, cleanup, and all other tasks done and still have five to ten minutes left for a closing circle.

1 **Post a chart of end-of-day tasks.** List the tasks students need to complete so they can refer to the list as they get ready for dismissal. (In the older elementary grades, consider asking students to help generate this list. Doing so can help children feel more invested in learning the end-of-day routines.)

However you create the list, keep it as short as possible. Consolidate similar details to end up with a general list that will apply to all students each day. A sample:

- Put homework and notices into folder and then into backpack.

- Pack up lunch box.

- Gather coat, gloves, hat, etc.

- Carefully flip your chair over onto your desk.

- Come to the closing circle.

For younger students, you might add photos to remind them what it looks like to pack up, clean up, and be ready for the end of the day.

2 **Assign and review homework earlier in the day.** Some teachers do this after a morning snack, right after lunch, or when students return from a special. If the class has a slice of time between subjects and specials, use it to assign homework instead of waiting until the end of the day.

3 **Assign and post classroom jobs.** Not only does this help ensure that the end of the day is organized and efficient, but it also gives children meaningful responsibilities as active participants in a classroom community.

You can come up with the jobs yourself or create them with students after the first week or so of school. Then rotate students through the jobs.

However you decide to create and assign jobs, be sure that the tasks genuinely contribute to the cleaning, organizing, and upkeep of the classroom and that everyone has a job to do. Also take the time to teach how to do each job (see "Model, Model, Model!" on page 18).

Finally, for jobs that take longer (such as stacking chairs), assign multiple students so that all jobs are finished at the same time.

Some ideas for classroom jobs:

- Pencil Sharpener
- Paper Monitor (passes out notices, worksheets, etc.)
- Chair Stacker(s)
- Chalkboard/Overhead Eraser
- Table/Desk Washer(s)
- Floor Checker (makes sure everything is off the floor)
- Computer Technician (shuts down computers)
- Librarian(s) (organizes classroom library)
- Plant Technician (waters plants)
- Animal Keeper (takes care of any classroom pets)
- Teacher Assistant (helps the teacher with any additional jobs)

4 **Note individual dismissal plans.** Make sure all students know where they're going that day and how (bus? after-school program? parent pickup?) before the closing circle begins. Many teachers use a small chart for this purpose.

⑤ Play a song. Play a piece of music while students are completing their class jobs and packing up. Try "So Long, Farewell" from the movie *The Sound of Music,* "See Ya Later, Alligator," or "Hit The Road, Jack." The length of the song should be the length of time it takes for students to complete their tasks and gather for the closing circle. As students get to know the song, it will become a pacing aid, with the end of the song a natural signal that their closing circle is about to begin.

⑥ Clarify the routines to yourself. To teach students how to carry out their end-of-day routines, you first need to clarify to yourself how each routine should look. Take a moment to visualize the details (you may even want to do a dry run). Some things to think about:

- How will I signal students to start these routines? Ring a chime? Use a hand signal? Something else?

- Should students do their class jobs first or pack up their personal belongings first?

- Will students flip up or stack the chairs?

- Will they leave their backpacks at their seats or in their cubbies during the closing circle or bring them to the circle?

16

- Is there room for children to put their backpacks behind them at the circle?

- How will students know when they should gather for the closing circle? After a song ends? When a timer goes off? When I turn off the lights?

Even though these seem like small details, it's important to think about them so that everyone will be clear on exactly what to do.

7 **Think about how to dismiss students from the closing circle.** Ask yourself these questions ahead of time:

- Will students line up at the door?

- Will they play a category game to line up (everyone whose middle name starts with A, B, or C may get in line, everyone whose middle name starts with D, E, or F may get in line, and so forth)? Or will you use some other method?

- Will students stay in the circle for bus announcements?

- What can children do while they wait? Perhaps play a quiet hand game?

Again, this may seem like a small detail, but the more you clarify your expectations, the more smoothly the end of the day will flow and the more time the class will have for a meaningful closing circle.

Model, Model, Model!

Once you've designed efficient tasks and routines, you need to carefully teach them to students so they'll know how to carry them out. Without this deliberate teaching, the most efficiently designed routines may trip students up and become time-consuming—because while you may have a clear picture of what you want students to do, they may not have the same mental image.

Interactive Modeling, a technique used in the *Responsive Classroom* approach to teaching (www.responsiveclassroom.org), is a simple and direct strategy for teaching routines (routines in general, not just those at the end of the day). Interactive Modeling allows students to see, hear, and experience exactly how to complete tasks. It includes seven quick steps:

1. Say what you will model and why.

2. Model the behavior.

3. Ask students what they noticed.

4. Invite one or more students to model.

5. Again, ask students what they noticed.

6. Have all students practice.

7. Provide feedback.

Following are two examples of the use of Interactive Modeling. To learn more about using this technique throughout the day, see *Interactive Modeling: A Powerful Technique for Teaching Children* by Margaret Berry Wilson, available from www.responsiveclassroom.org.

18

Interactive Modeling: How to Stack Chairs

STEP	MIGHT LOOK/SOUND LIKE
1. Say what you will model and why.	"At the end of the day, we need to put the chairs on the desks to help the custodian. It's important to do this safely and carefully. I'm going to stack this chair. See what you notice."
2. Model the behavior.	Stack the chair carefully. Do not narrate as you model.
3. Ask students what they noticed.	"What did you notice about what I did?" Students might respond, "You used both hands" or "You moved the chair slowly." If needed, ask questions such as "What were my eyes doing?" and "How hard did I put my chair down?" to prompt students to name all the important aspects of safe chair stacking.
4. Invite one or more students to model.	"Who else would like to show us safe chair stacking? OK, let's all watch Brooke and Mary."
5. Again, ask students what they noticed.	"What did you see Brooke and Mary do?" Students might respond, "They were quiet" or "They kept their eyes on their chairs so they didn't bump into each other."
6. Have all students practice.	"Now we're all going to practice stacking a chair. I'll watch to see that you do the things your classmates and I just modeled."
7. Provide feedback.	"You stacked your chairs safely and carefully. I saw slow movements. I saw people avoiding bumping others and putting chairs down gently."

19

Interactive Modeling: How to Respond to the Signal for Quiet Attention

Using a calm signal such as a chime or a raised hand to get children's attention is among a teacher's most important classroom management techniques. It's a highly efficient and respectful way to get children's attention throughout the day, but especially at the end of the day, when students are tired and tend to have trouble focusing. Teach children that when you give the signal, they should stop what they're doing, get quiet, and look at you to hear your directions.

STEP	MIGHT LOOK/SOUND LIKE
1. Say what you will model and why.	"At times when I need to get your attention, I'll ring a chime. Madelyn will pretend to be the teacher and ring the chime. I'll be a student. Watch me to notice what I do when the chime rings." (Arrange ahead of time for Madelyn to help with this modeling.)
2. Model the behavior.	Walk around the room. When you hear the chime, stop moving and look at Madelyn. Do not narrate as you model.
3. Ask students what they noticed.	"What did you notice about what I did?" Students might answer, "You stopped moving" or "You turned your head to look at Madelyn."
4. Invite one or more students to model.	"Who else would like to show us what to do when the chime rings? OK, let's all watch carefully as Sandhya and Ian respond when I ring the chime." ▶

STEP	MIGHT LOOK/SOUND LIKE
5. Again, ask students what they noticed.	"What did you see Sandhya and Ian do?" Students might say, "They stopped their conversation" or "They turned to look at you."
6. Have all students practice.	"Looks like you're all ready to try responding to the signal. Turn to your neighbor and tell him or her about your favorite place, and when you hear the chime, stop and look at me. I'll be watching for all of you to do what your classmates and I modeled."
7. Provide feedback.	"You all stopped and looked quickly. This will help us throughout the school day to be ready for learning."

A Last Thought

Given how packed school schedules are, doing one more thing may seem impossible. What we can tell you is that the investment in closing circles comes back to you tenfold. In the years we've been using closing circles in our classrooms, we've found students, and ourselves, leaving school with energy and enthusiasm rather than fatigue or discouragement. Other teachers who use this practice report the same. We invite you to discover for yourself what a difference closing circles can make.

21

Activity Finder

Use these tables to find activities
that fit your class's needs.
Or simply browse the book
for suitable choices.

Grades K-2

Grades 3-6

Activities
for Grades

K-6

1, 2, 3, Pop!

Grades

K-6

Materials needed:

Skills reinforced:

recall, counting, public speaking

1 **Name a topic** for children to take turns sharing about, such as something they're looking forward to tomorrow.

2 **Students count off:** "1, 2, 3" around the circle.

3 **The fourth person stands up** as she says "Pop!" and then shares. For example, "I'm looking forward to music class tomorrow."

4 **The rest of the group says** (in unison) "Good-bye, [student's name]."

5 **The next person in the circle begins the counting again,** starting with 1. (People who have popped up remain standing and do not participate in the counting.) Continue until everyone has had a chance to pop and share information.

More sample sharing topics for Step 1

➤ Something students learned today

➤ Something that went well for students today

➤ Something from the school day that students will tell family members about tonight

➤ One way students saw the class following a class rule today

➤ A friendly, kind behavior students saw at recess or lunch today

TIP

If the dismissal line is close to the closing circle spot, you could have students line up after they pop.

Variation

In Step 1, students skip count (for example: 1, 4, 7, 10, etc.) or use some other counting method, depending on their grade and skill level.

31

Around-the-Circle Sharing

Grades

K-6

Materials needed:

Skills reinforced:

taking turns, listening, public speaking

1 **Ask a question** that gets students to think back on their learning that day, such as "What's one new thing you learned today?"

2 **Each student gives a brief response** to the question. (Decide and let students know ahead of time whether they may pass.)

More sample questions for Step 1

➤ What was one of the best parts of your day?

➤ What are you looking forward to doing tomorrow? After school? This weekend?

➤ What was one way you followed our rules today?

➤ What new strategy did you try in math today?

TIP

Use Interactive Modeling (see page 18) to show children how to share one idea briefly.

Around the World

Materials needed:

Skills reinforced:

taking turns, making eye contact, using non-English words and phrases

1 **Choose a non-English word for good-bye.** Or ask a student to choose. For example, the word could be "Sayonara" (Japanese).

2 **Student 1 turns to face his neighbor** —Emily, for example—makes eye contact, smiles, and says, "Sayonara, Emily."

3 **Emily turns to face the next child** and says good-bye in the same way, using the same "good-bye" word.

4 **Continue around the circle** until everyone has had a chance to say good-bye.

Good-bye, so long, and similar terms from around the world (search online or ask native speakers for help with pronunciation and proper usage)

→ Ma'a as-salaamah (Arabic)
→ Zai jian (Mandarin Chinese)
→ Au revoir (French)
→ Auf Wiedersehen (German)
→ Aloha (Hawaiian)
→ Shalom (Hebrew)
→ Namaste (Hindi)
→ Arrivederci (Italian)
→ Sayonara (Japanese)
→ Do widzenia (Polish)
→ Da svedanya (Russian)
→ Adiós (Spanish)
→ Kwaheri (Swahili)
→ Selavu (Telugu—spoken in Southern India)
→ "See you later" gesture (American Sign Language—point to own eyes with index and middle finger, then point with index finger to person you're talking to)

Ball Toss Good-bye

Materials needed:

Foam or other kind of ball suitable for tossing indoors

Skills reinforced:

taking turns, gentle and controlled tossing, hand-eye coordination

1 **Choose a child to go first (let's say Omar).** He picks a student across the circle (Lorena) by pointing or saying her name. Once Lorena is looking at him, Omar says, "Good-bye, Lorena" and gently tosses, rolls, or bounces a ball to her.

2 **Lorena replies, "Good-bye, Omar,"** chooses a different person across the circle (Natalie), and says "Good-bye, Natalie," passing the ball to her.

3 **Continue in this way** until each child has been told good-bye. The activity ends when the ball returns to the student who started.

Variation for grades 3–6

After Step 3, challenge students to pass the ball around one more time silently in the same or reverse order. Or add one or two more balls so that several are going around one after another in the same order.

Circle of Hands

1 **Students stand** with their right arm extended toward the middle of the circle. Their left arm stays down by their side.

2 **Students make a fist** with their right hand, palm side down, and extend their thumb. They put their thumb inside the fist of the person to their left, creating a large, tight circle.

3 **The class does a quick cheer,** such as "Go, Team!" while raising all arms up in the air and then breaking apart.

More sample cheers for Step 3

- ➛ Wow!
- ➛ Yay, friends!
- ➛ Good night!
- ➛ Peace out!

Or have the class make up their own cheer.

TIP

Use Interactive Modeling (see page 18) to teach students how to gently hold onto their neighbor's thumb.

Compliment Circle

Materials needed:

Skills reinforced:

observation, recall, using descriptive language, giving and receiving compliments, public speaking

1 **Tell the class early in the day** that in closing circle they'll be complimenting classmates on their positive behaviors. Tell students to look throughout the day for things such as people making friendly lunch conversation or helping others solve a math problem.

2 **Start the closing circle by modeling** a respectful compliment. For example, turn toward a student, look at him, and say "You invited someone to join a game at recess today" with a friendly face and voice.

3 **A student starts by complimenting** the person to his right. For example, "Julia, I noticed how you held the door open at lunch today."

4 **Julia says** "Thank you" and nothing else, and the compliment giver says "You're welcome."

5 **Continue around the circle.** If you have time, do a second round in the reverse direction.

TIPS

Save this activity for midyear, when students are more comfortable talking about each other's behavior.

For grades 3–6, start by using pre-made compliment cards (see next page) to give students safe practice in giving compliments. Later, they can come up with their own compliments.

CONTINUED ▶

Reproducible Compliment Cards

Make enough cards for each student to have one, plus a few extra. When it's their turn, students draw a card, decide whom the compliment applies to, and place the card in front of that classmate. Each student should receive only one card.

You helped someone today.	You showed responsibility today.
You showed cooperation today.	You showed self-control today.

You showed kindness today.	You took a learning risk today.
You were a good friend today.	You were respectful today.
You shared today.	You were a good listener today.

Did You Know?

Grades

K-6

Materials needed:

Skills reinforced:

synthesizing, recall, taking turns, public speaking

1 **Choose a social or academic topic** the class is learning about. For example, "friendliness" or "butterflies."

- - - - - - - - - -

2 **Students take turns completing** this question: "Did you know [topic] [fact about the topic]?" For example:

* "Did you know butterflies come out of a chrysalis?"

* "Did you know that being friendly means using kind body language when a person makes a mistake?"

- - - - - - - - - -

3 **The whole class responds** enthusiastically, "We do now!" to each question.

- - - - - - - - - -

44

TIPS

For grades K–2, it's best to save
this activity for midyear, when students
have had practice listening
and staying on topic.

Write out the sentence frame
for students to look at as
they do this activity.

45

Farewell Snake

1 **Students stand.** Student 1 steps inside the circle, turns to student 2 on her left, and says good-bye to him.

2 **Student 1 continues walking** around inside the circle saying good-bye to each classmate.

3 **Student 2 follows** behind student 1, also saying good-bye to each classmate. The inside line grows as each student follows by joining the end of the line and saying good-bye to everyone in the circle.

4 **Students line up** to leave the classroom after saying good-bye or return to their original spot in the circle. (Tell the class ahead of time what you want them to do.)

TIP

Remind students to use inside voices.
Otherwise, this activity can get loud.

Variations

➤ Let student 1 choose a respectful gesture
with which to say good-bye (for example,
a wave, a handshake, or a salute). Everyone then uses that gesture.

➤ Connect to the curriculum by finding out
how people say good-bye in a country the
class is studying and use that remark or
gesture.

Fist to Five: How Did You Do?

Grades

K-6

Materials
needed:

Skills
reinforced:

self-assessment

1   **Ask students** how they think they are doing individually on an academic or social skill. For example, "How do you think your science project went today?"

2   **Students respond** by holding up zero to five fingers. Zero (a fist) means "I didn't make much progress." Five means "I made a lot of progress." (If they're unsure or don't want to share, they may pass.)

3   **If many students show zeros and ones,** explore with the class the next day what additional teaching you should do. In the moment, you might say, "I'm going to think more about this, and tomorrow we can plan together how to make things better."

More sample questions for Step 1

➤ How did your work with paragraphs go in writing workshop today?

➤ How did you do today with our goal of talking to someone you don't usually talk to at lunch?

➤ Think back to when we made number sentences today. How did you do with representing the numbers clearly?

➤ We've been working hard at including everyone during recess. How did you do today?

TIPS

Limit your question to a specific skill or project the class is working on.

· · · · · · · · · · · ·

Ask children to reflect on their own performance rather than that of the group.

Give This Group a Hand

Materials needed:

Skills reinforced:

touching gently, keeping rhythm

1 **Students stand** in a circle.

2 **Students chant the following:**
(Give a pause at the dashes.)

We're gonna give—this—group a hand.

We're gonna give this group a hand.
(Clap twice.)

We're gonna give—this—group a hand.

We're gonna give this group a hand.
(Clap twice.)

So raise your hands up in the air.
(Raise hands.)

And pat your neighbor—right there.
(Gently pat the shoulder of the neighbor on the left and on the right.)

Use Interactive Modeling (see page 18)
to teach students what a gentle pat looks like.

Good-bye Cadence

Grades

K-6

Materials needed:

Skills reinforced:

keeping rhythm, reading

Send students off on a high note with this rousing call-and-response chant.

Leader: *I don't know but I've been told*

Group: *I don't know but I've been told*

Leader: *This school day is about to fold*

Group: *This school day is about to fold*

Leader: *We worked and played our best all day*

Group: *We worked and played our best all day*

Leader: *But now it's time for us to say*

Group: *But now it's time for us to say*

Leader: *Sound off*

Group: *Good-bye*

Leader: *Sound off*

Group: *School friends*

Leader: *Bring it on down now* (whisper the rest of the chant)

Group: *Good-bye, school friends*

All: *Bye, bye!*

Post the words of the chant so students
can refer to them if needed.

Variation

Instead of "school friends" insert any two-
syllable name for the group, such as "first grade,"
"classmates," or "readers." Or ask your students
for suggestions!

Hand Hugs

1 **Students stand, cross their arms** in front of themselves, and join hands with the people on either side.

2 **Choose a person to start.** That child gently squeezes *one* neighbor's hand.

3 **Each child waits for a gentle hand squeeze** and then gently squeezes the hand of the next child, sending the "hug" around the circle.

Use Interactive Modeling (see page 18)
to teach gentle hand-squeezing.

• • • • • • • • • • • •

Save this one for later in the year,
when students are more comfortable
with physical contact.

Variation

Teach students the Shel Silverstein poem
"Hug O' War." They can memorize the poem
and recite it as the hand hugs go around.

I Used to Think . . .

1. **Choose a topic** that students are currently studying.

· · · · · · · · · ·

2. **Students fill in the blanks** in the following sentence about their new learning on that topic:

I used to think _____, but now I know _____.

For example:

* "I used to think fractions were hard, but now I think they are just parts of something."

* "I used to think whales were fish, but now I know they breathe air."

· · · · · · · · · ·

It may help to post the sentence frame.

Variation

Depending on how much time you have, you can do this as an around-the-circle sharing or a partner sharing, or just call on a few students to share aloud.

Inside, Outside Circles

Grades

K-6

Materials needed:

Skills reinforced:

taking turns,
voicing an opinion,
listening

1 **Students stand and count off by twos.** The ones stay where they are and each two turns to face a one, creating an inside circle facing an outside circle.

* * * * * * * * *

2 **Pose a reflection question, such as** "What was one thing you enjoyed about your work in _____ today?" or "What helped us have a good inside recess today?" Students take turns answering the question with the partner they're facing.

* * * * * * * * * *

3 **Students in the outside circle move to their right** and face a new partner. Pose a new question and have partners share their answers with each other. Continue with as many new questions and partners as you have time for.

* * * * * * * * *

More sample questions for Step 2

→ Today, when someone at home asks you, "What did you do at school today?" what's one thing you can tell them about your work?

→ Think back over our work in science today. What's something you're still thinking or wondering about?

Just Like Me

Grades

K-6

Materials needed:

Skills reinforced:

listening,
assertiveness,
self-awareness

1 **The leader (you or a student) stands** in the center of the circle. Everyone else sits.

2 **The leader says a statement** about something positive that happened that day, such as "I learned something new today." Everyone to whom the statement applies stands up and says "Just like me!" and then sits down again.

3 **The leader says another statement,** and group members again respond.

4 **The activity continues** through a number of statements.

More sample statements for Step 2

→ I did something I was proud of today.

→ I had fun learning about [academic or social topic] today.

→ I was kind to someone today.

→ I took on a challenge today.

→ I solved a problem today.

→ I was excited about something today.

→ I worked with someone different today.

→ I accomplished something today.

→ I'm looking forward to something tomorrow.

TIP

If you're struggling to come up with enough statements, open it up to your students. They're bound to have some good ideas.

61

Linger

Chanting or singing a comforting song

makes for a simple, effective closing circle activity. This one is adapted from the children's camp song "Linger." (Search online to hear the tune.)

Mm-mm, I want to linger

Mm-mm, a little longer

Mm-mm, a little longer here with you.

Mm-mm, and as the years go by,

Mm-mm, I'll think of you and sigh.

Mm-mm, this is good night and not good-bye.

Post the words of the song so students can refer to them if needed.

Maître d'

1. **Call out,** "Table for [a number from 2 through 4]."

2. **Students quickly assemble** in small groups with that number of members.

3. **Ask a question** for children to answer in their group or give a topic for them to discuss. For example, "Which way of practicing spelling words works best for you?"

4. **Call out another table number** after all students have had time to share in their small groups. Students form new small groups based on the new number.

More sample questions for Step 3

➤ What could we do to welcome our new classmate next week?

➤ What's your favorite time of the school day?

➤ What's one thing we could do to make our field trip go well tomorrow?

➤ Who's your favorite (or least favorite) character in our read-aloud?

Partner Sharing

1 **Students pair up with a buddy** (the next student in the circle or a buddy you assign).

2 **Ask the class a question** that gets them thinking about something they learned during the past day or week. For example, "What's one thing you learned today about yourself [our class, our school, a subject you are studying]?"

3 **Students share their answer** with their partner (if needed, specify which partner should go first).

4 **Student volunteers tell the class** one thing their partners shared, if time allows.

More sample questions for Step 2

➤ What's one surprising thing that happened to you this week?

➤ What's one thing you're looking forward to this weekend?

TIP

This activity works best after the class has built a sense of trust and community—usually midyear.

Popcorn Sharing

Grades

K-6

Materials
needed:

Skills
reinforced:

assertiveness,
taking turns,
self-control,
listening, public
speaking

1 **Ask the class a question** about their learning, such as "What book are you reading right now?"

2 **Students "pop up"** (stand up) to answer. They do this without raising hands or using any predetermined order. Instead, they listen carefully to know when it's a good time to jump in.

3 **If two children stand together,** they sit down and the class tries again.

4 **Ask a new question** when you think enough children have shared. (Everyone needn't answer every question. But you may want to limit children to popping up just once for each question.)

More sample questions for Step 1

➤ What's one thing you learned about _____ (any academic content the class is studying) this week?

➤ When were you a good listener today?

➤ What's something you did this week that you are proud of?

➤ What story are you working on in writing this week?

TIP

To minimize competition, save this activity until the class has established a sense of trust and community—usually midyear.

Thumb Gauge: Did You Like It?

Grades

K-6

Materials needed:

Skills reinforced:

self-awareness, voicing an opinion

1 **Ask students** whether they personally liked or agreed with something from the school day. For example, "Did you like the dice game we played today?" or "In today's read-aloud, do you agree with the coach's decision to cancel all the away games?"

2 **Students respond silently,** using their thumb to show if they liked or agreed with something.

* Thumb up = yes
* Thumb in the middle = not sure
* Thumb down = no

3 **Summarize** aloud the responses that you see.

More sample questions for Step 1

➤ Did you like the story we read today?

➤ Are you excited about our upcoming field trip?

➤ Do you agree with [a conclusion from a newspaper article, a choice that a character made, a weather prediction, etc.]?

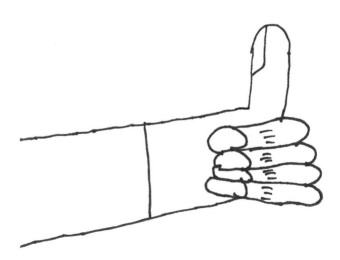

Today Is Friday!

These lyrics were written by Jill Whitacre, a teacher at West Shore Junior-Senior High School in Melbourne, Florida.

Grades

K-6

Materials needed:

Skills reinforced:

recall, counting, public speaking

Chant these lyrics for an energizing end to the week. Or sing the words to the tune of "La Cucaracha" (search online to hear many renditions of the tune). Pause briefly at each dash.

Today is Fri—day (raise an arm up in the air with closed fist)

Today is Fri—day (raise an arm up in the air with closed fist)

Da, da, da, da, da, da, da (twist upper body while keeping feet planted)

Today is Fri—day (raise an arm up in the air with closed fist)

Today is Fri—day (raise an arm up in the air with closed fist)

See you back here on Mon-day Cha, cha, cha! (wiggle hips from side to side)

Post the words of the chant so students can refer to them if needed.

Variations

➤ Do this on other days of the week. Simply change Friday to the appropriate day.

➤ Ask students to invent new movements to go along with the various days of the week.

The Weekend Is Near

Grades

K-6

Materials needed:

Skills reinforced:

taking turns, nonverbal expression

Try this active call-and-response chant to help students transition to the weekend.

Group:

Hello, [name of child being greeted]!
The weekend is near. (Group waves while chanting.)

What are you gonna do (Group points at person being greeted.)

When it really gets here? (Group points down at floor.)

Child being greeted:

I'm gonna [action], [action], [action]. (Child names and pantomimes one action three times.)

Group:

He's gonna [action], [action], [action]. (Group repeats and pantomimes same action three times.)

74

Before doing this activity,
you might want to brainstorm possible
responses and pantomimes.

What Do You Remember?

Grades

K-6

Materials
needed:

Popsicle sticks, can

Skills
reinforced:

recall, careful
observation, public
speaking

1 **Write different parts of the day** (arrival, lunch, math, specials, read-aloud, and so forth) on Popsicle sticks and place the sticks in a can before the closing circle.

2 **Pass the can around the circle.** Each student takes a turn pulling out a stick and saying one thing she noticed during that part of the day. For example:

* Arrival stick: "I noticed my bus was late this morning because of all the snow."

* Lunch stick: "I noticed the lunch room was really noisy today."

* Specials stick: "I noticed we all remembered our books for library today."

76

* Science stick: "I noticed that the bean plants closest to the windows are the tallest."

* Math stick: "I noticed that we have lots of triangle shapes in our room."

It's OK for students to repeat what others have said.

● ● ● ● ● ● ● ● ● ● ● ● ●

T I P

If you don't have Popsicle sticks, index cards in a basket would also work fine.

Activities
for Grades

K-2

Children, Children, What Do You Say?

Grades

K-2

Materials needed:

Skills reinforced:

recall, keeping rhythm, public speaking

1 **Establish a beat** by clapping your hands once, your thighs once, and so forth, keeping the rhythm going.

2 **The group chants the following words,** clapping hands on bold syllables and thighs on the others.

*Children, children, **what** do you **say**?* (pat thighs after *say*)

***What** was your **favorite thing** today?*

3 **Students take turns saying** their favorite thing from that day while trying to keep the clapping rhythm. This may not work for all students—and that's OK. The point is for everyone to participate and for the class to have fun together.

Five Senses

Materials needed:

Five Senses cards, basket or box

Skills reinforced:

taking turns, synthesizing, awareness of the five senses

1 **Prepare cards showing the five senses** as well as several free choice cards (use the reproducibles at right or have students make their own). Put these cards into a basket or box that can be passed around the circle.

2 **Each student in turn takes out a card** and recalls something from the day that relates to the card. For example, "I SMELLED our pizza baking in the oven at lunch" or "I HEARD Mary say something kind to Anna during Morning Meeting."

3 **The student then puts the card back** and passes the basket or box to the next person.

82

Taste

Smell

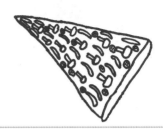

See

Hear

Touch

Free Choice

(Choose any one of
the five senses.)

Good-bye Signs

Grades

K-2

Materials needed:

Skills reinforced:

taking turns, making eye contact

1 **Student 1 turns to face student 2,** makes eye contact, smiles, and says good-bye—for example, "See you tomorrow, Oscar"— with a simple gesture such as a wave.

2 **Oscar then turns to face the next student** and says good-bye with the same words and gesture.

3 **Continue around the circle** until everyone has had a chance to say good-bye.

More sample good-bye gestures for this activity

➤ Salute

➤ Bow

➤ Thumbs-up

➤ Peace sign

➤ Handshake

➤ Fist bump

Or brainstorm other respectful good-bye gestures with students.

► TIP ◄

Save handshakes and fist bumps for
a little later in the year, when students have
gotten to know each other and are more
comfortable with physical contact.

85

Hot Pepper

Materials needed:

a small ball or beanbag

Skills reinforced:

self-control, listening, public speaking

1 **Students close their eyes.**

· · · · · · · · ·

2 **Give a small ball to one student,** who passes the ball quickly to the next person while saying "Hot!" Students continue to pass the ball around the circle.

· · · · · · · · · ·

3 **Turn your back and call out "Pepper!"** as the ball is being passed.

· · · · · · · · ·

4 **The person holding the ball** when you call "Pepper!" answers a question from you, such as "What was your favorite part of today?" and then takes one step back from the circle or lines up for dismissal. (Tell the children before you start what you want them to do.) Continue until all students have answered a question.

· · · · · · · · · ·

More sample questions for Step 4

➤ What do you need to remember to bring back to school tomorrow?

➤ What's one thing you can tell someone at home about what you did at school today?

➤ What's one thing from today's learning that you'd like to know more about?

➤ What's one word you'd use to describe the kind of day you had?

Make a Gesture

Grades

K-2

Materials needed:

Skills reinforced:

taking turns,
self-assessment,
silent expression

1 **Students pair up with a buddy** (the next student in the circle or a buddy you assign).

. . . .

2 **Students think of a silent gesture** to represent their thoughts or feelings about the day (for example, they could point to their brain to show they're thinking about something or do a triumphant fist pump to show they accomplished something hard). Students give a thumbs-up when they're ready.

. . . .

3 **Each person shows** his silent gesture, taking turns around the circle.

. . . .

TIP

Brainstorm a few gestures with students.
Or just demonstrate two or three
possible gestures and have students
choose among those.

Variation

Have students give a sound or word in addition to (or instead of) a gesture. For example, saying "Yippee" while throwing arms in the air to show they're excited about something or "Hmmm" to show they're still puzzling over something they studied.

Make a Wish

Grades

K-2

Materials needed:

Skills reinforced:

envisioning, moving safely and carefully

1 **Each student thinks of** a personal school-related wish and whispers the wish into her cupped hands. (Wishes stay private.)

2 **Students then close one hand** as though they are holding the wish inside it and raise the closed hand into the air to signal readiness.

3 **Give a signal** when all students have a hand raised. Students open their closed hand while gently blowing upward to release the wish into the air.

90

Make New Friends

Grades

K-2

Materials needed:

Skills reinforced:

keeping rhythm,
singing together,
reading

Bring even rough days to a positive end
with friendship songs like this traditional
one. (Search online to hear the tune.)

Make new friends,
but keep the old.

One is silver,
the other is gold.

A circle is round,
it has no end.

That's how long
I want to be your friend.

► TIP ◄

Post the words of the song so students
can refer to them if needed.

The More We Get Together

Grades

K-2

Materials needed:

Skills reinforced:

keeping rhythm, singing together, reading

Simply chanting or singing together can bring the day to a soothing and positive end, especially for young children. Search online to hear the tune for this traditional children's song.

The more we get together,
Together, together,

The more we get together,
The happier we'll be.

For your friends are my friends,
And my friends are your friends.

Oh, the more we get together,
The happier we'll be!

Post the words of the song so students
can refer to them if needed.

Quiet Think Time

**Materials
needed:**

**Skills
reinforced:**

recall, thinking
quietly, listening,
public speaking

1 **Students close their eyes** and get in a comfortable position. They may lie down if there's space.

· · · · · · · · · · ·

2 **Say a word or short phrase** to prompt students to think about what they learned that day, such as "writing workshop," "new recess game," or "inviting lunch partners." Give them some silent think time.

· · · · · · · · · · ·

3 **Give one or two more prompts.** After the last prompt, invite students to share one thing they thought about during the silent think times—something important to remember, a connection they made to something else, a question they have, etc.

· · · · · · · · · · ·

Variation

Invite students to share after each prompt.

94

Remember When?

1 **Student 1 turns to student 2** and asks, "Remember when ... ?" and inserts something he remembers from that school day. For example, "Remember when we used small blocks and added more and more to our piles?"

2 **Student 2 says,** "I do remember that!" and then turns to student 3 and repeats "Remember when ... ," inserting something different that she remembers about the day.

3 **Continue around the circle.**

95

Special Delivery

Materials needed:

pencils, scrap paper, clipboards, "mailbox" (a small box or basket)

Skills reinforced:

recall, illustrating an idea

1. **Give each student a pencil,** a piece of paper, and a clipboard.

2. **Students draw a quick picture** of something they learned that day and put their pictures into a "mailbox"—a small box or basket in the middle of the circle.

3 **Acting as a postmaster, deliver** (randomly pass out) a drawing to each student.

· · · · · · · · · · · · ·

4 **Students look at the drawing** they received and walk around trying to match it to the artist so they can hear about what that person learned.

· · · · · · · · · · · · ·

97

Through the Looking Glass

Grades

K-2

Materials needed:

a pair of glasses (clown glasses, big sunglasses, binoculars)

Skills reinforced:

recall, public speaking

1 **Pass a pair of large glasses around** the circle.

2 **Each student puts the glasses on** and names something positive he saw that day. For example, "I saw Reva walking in the hallway" or "I saw Bien swinging safely on the swings at recess."

98

A Wish and Two Stars

Materials needed:

Skills reinforced:

self-awareness, self-assessment, goal setting

1 **Students think about** two things they did well today or this week (the stars) and one thing they wish to do better tomorrow or next time (the wish).

2 **Choose one of these ways** for students to share their wish and two stars:

* Tell them to just one partner.

* Write them down for posting on the wall or for you to read privately.

* "Pop" share one at a time without a predetermined order (see Popcorn Sharing on page 68).

Consider the class's trust in one another and their communication skills as you choose the sharing method.

Activities
for Grades

3-6

ABC Summary

Materials needed:

chart paper, whiteboard, or interactive whiteboard

Skills reinforced:

summarizing, synthesizing

1 **List all the letters of the alphabet** on the chart or board.

. . . .

2 **Choose a topic** that the students are learning about. Have students call out a word or phrase related to the topic that begins with each letter of the alphabet.

Example:

Topic: **Oceans**

A tlantic
B ottlenose Dolphin
C oral Reef
D iver
E el
F an Coral
G
H igh Tide

and so on.

. . . .

It's not necessary to come up with
an idea for every letter of the alphabet.
If students get stuck on a letter,
move on to the next.

Variation

Have students work in small groups to generate ideas before doing this activity as a whole
class. Each group can focus on just a few
letters.

Amazing Analogies

Grades

3-6

Materials needed:

Skills reinforced:

creative thinking, making analogies, public speaking

1 **Think of a topic** that students have been learning about.

2 **Ask,** "How is [topic] like [a common classroom item or tool]?

Examples:

How is multiplication like a stapler?
How is friendship like a pencil box?
(Give students think time.)

3 **Take multiple ideas.** Have students answer by saying, "[Topic] is like [a classroom item or tool] because [reason]." For example: "Multiplication is like a stapler because it's a way of attaching numbers together quickly." Or "Friendship is like a pencil box because it's filled with special treasures."

Variation

Have students pair up and brainstorm together about the analogy. Then have pairs share their ideas with the class.

Beat the Clock

Materials needed:

paper, pencil, timer or clock

Skills reinforced:

envisioning, cooperating

1 **Students form teams of three to five.** Give each team a piece of paper and a pencil. Each team designates one student to be the recorder. You serve as the timekeeper.

· · · · · · · · · ·

2 **Ask a question about school,** such as "How did you use your pencil to help you learn today?" Teams write down as many ways as possible before time is up. (To build suspense and help children focus, don't tell them how much time they'll have.)

· · · · · · · · · ·

3 **Teams take turns sharing their lists.**

· · · · · · · · · ·

More sample questions for Step 2

➤ What are the steps in [a classroom procedure]?

➤ What did you see on the field trip today?

➤ How might you help a friend on the playground?

➤ How can you use clay to help you learn?

➤ What are ____ facts you learned from our unit on [a unit of study]? (You designate the number of facts.)

Cooperative Sentences

Grades

3-6

Materials needed:

sticky notes, pencils

Skills reinforced:

cooperation, summarizing, using descriptive language

1 **Students write one word** that describes their day on a sticky note before they come to the circle. For example, they might write "active," "challenging," or "fun."

2 **Students go around the circle sharing** their words with the class.

3 **Groups of three or four students then work together** to create a sentence that describes the work they did that day, incorporating all the words in their group. For example:

Words: *long, fun, learning, busy*

Sentence: *During this long, busy day, we had fun learning together.*

Or

Some of us had a busy, fun learning day, but some of us just felt the day was long.

4 **Go around the circle again** with each group sharing their sentences aloud.

109

Hard Workers

Grades

3-6

Materials needed:

Skills reinforced:

listening, public speaking

1 **Name one thing** the class has worked hard on this week. For example, "We worked hard on our self-portraits."

2 **A student repeats your statement** and adds one of his own. For example, "Not only did we work hard on our self-portraits, but we also worked hard on our 3-D maps."

3 **The next student repeats** the last statement and adds one of her own: "Not only did we work hard on our 3-D maps, but we also worked hard on our 'I Have a Dream' poems."

4 **Continue** until no one has anything more to add, or until you're out of time.

Before starting the activity,
briefly brainstorm with students
some recent projects and assignments
they've been working on.

Variations

→ Challenge students to repeat all the previous statements. For example, the third student in the example here would say, "Not only did we work hard on our self-portraits, our 3-D maps, and our 'I Have a Dream' poems, but also our . . ."

→ Instead of realistic statements, have everyone make exaggerated or fanciful statements, such as "We worked hard on our invisibility cloak invention" or "We worked hard building our asteroid deflector."

The Last Word

Materials needed:

chart paper,
whiteboard,
or interactive
whiteboard,
marker

Skills reinforced:

synthesizing,
summarizing

1 **Choose a key word** related to a topic that students have been learning about.

· · · · · · · · ·

2 **Write the word vertically** on a board or chart.

· · · · · · · · ·

3 **Students brainstorm words or phrases** relating to the topic for each letter. It's OK to leave a letter blank if no one has an idea for it. For example:

A steroids

S tars

T

R otation of the earth

O rbit

N eptune

O

M ercury

Y ellow like the sun

· · · · · · · · ·

TIP

Start with words that encompass broad topics, such as astronomy. This gives students a wide range of possible ideas to suggest.

Later, add challenge by using narrower topics—for example, Jupiter instead of astronomy.

Pass the Mask

Grades

3-6

Materials needed:

Skills reinforced:

self-expression,
empathizing,
taking turns

1 **Student 1 makes a face** to show how she's feeling at the end of the day and turns to student 2, thus "passing" her expression to him.

2 **Student 2 mirrors back** the expression. He then makes a face of his own to show how he's feeling and turns to student 3 to pass that expression to her.

3 **Continue around the circle** until everyone's had a chance to show an expression.

114

If time is short, have just a few students
each take a turn at making an expression
and have the whole class copy it
back to them.

· · · · · · · · · · · ·

If you're unsure of the cause of a student's
sad or angry face, follow up with her
privately to see if you can help.

Pluses and Wishes

Grades

3-6

Materials needed:

paper or index cards, pencil

Skills reinforced:

envisioning, writing

1 **Give each student** a piece of paper or an index card and a pencil.

2 **Ask students to write any number** of positives or "pluses" about their day on the left side. Some pluses might be:

* I really liked our new morning meeting greeting.

* I figured out the math problem I had trouble with last week.

* Using clay in art class was cool!

116

3 **Ask students to write** one wish for school tomorrow on the right side. Some wishes might be:

* I wish we had more time for silent reading.

* I hope I get a chance to work with a lot of partners.

* I wish I didn't sit by the window.

* I hope we get a chance to learn more about geometry.

4 **Collect students' papers** as they leave the classroom. Read them privately and adjust the next day's teaching as appropriate.

Variation

Invite students to read one "plus" aloud to the class.

117

Question of the Day

Materials needed:

prepared index cards with questions, basket or box

Skills reinforced:

cooperation, recall

1 **Write some questions about the day** on index cards before the closing circle. Examples: "What three ways did we follow our rules today?" or "What are some things you could look at under the microscopes tomorrow?" Put these cards into a basket or box that can be passed around the circle.

2 **Students form pairs or small teams** of three to five. One student in each group selects a card and reads it aloud to the rest of his group. The group works together to come up with answers.

3 **Ask each group to share their answers** with the whole class, if time allows.

More sample questions for Step 1

➤ What's one math problem you worked on today?

➤ What's [fact from a unit]? (For example, "What's the capital of New Hampshire?")

➤ What are two ways you saw classmates taking care of themselves today? Helping others? Showing kindness?

Variation

Instead of giving each group a different question, pose a single question for all groups to answer.

Snowball

Materials needed:

paper, pencils

Skills reinforced:

taking turns, gentle tossing, writing, reflection

1 **Give each student** a half piece of paper and a pencil.

· · · · · · · · · ·

2 **Ask the class a question about their day,** such as "What went well for you today?" Or give them a statement to complete, such as "A highlight for me today was _____ ." Students write their answers on their paper.

· · · · · · · · · ·

3 **Students crumple their paper into a ball.** On the count of three, all students gently toss their paper into the middle of the circle.

· · · · · · · · · ·

4 **Everyone then collects one crumpled "snowball"** from the pile. Going around the circle, students share what's written on the "snowball" they have in their hand.

· · · · · · · · · ·

Model how everyone in the group can safely collect snowballs at the same time.

Variation

In Step 3, students toss and retrieve snow-balls several times, thus more thoroughly shuffling the pile in a fun way.

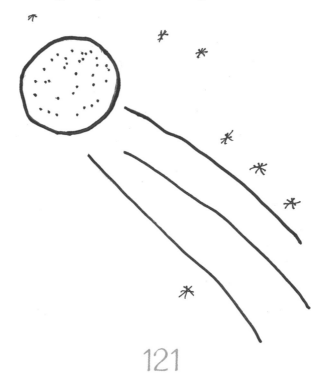

Street Signs

Grades

3-6

Materials needed:

whiteboards
(or scrap paper
and clipboards),
markers

Skills reinforced:

recall, making
connections

1. **Pass out a whiteboard** (or a clipboard and scrap paper) and a marker to each student.

2. **Students come up with a street sign** or billboard that highlights something they learned that day. For example, "Coming Soon: Double-Digit Multiplication!" or "Take the next exit for cool new recess games."

3. **Students hold up their signs** in turn for everyone to read silently.

Write down the lines students come up with. They'll be a great addition to your class webpage or parent newsletter!

Variation for grades K–6

Pass a rolled-up newspaper around the circle. When students get the newspaper, they turn to their neighbor, say, "Here's the news!" and state a "headline" for the day, such as "Mrs. Ferron's Class Subtracts Three-Digit Numbers!" or "Shreya Conquers a New Novel!"

Tell Me This . . .

Materials needed:

Skills reinforced:

recall, listening, cooperation, public speaking

1 **Prepare some questions** before the closing circle related to things that happened that day. For example:

* "Today in science we practiced making observations. Tell me this: What's one observation you made?"

* "We worked in groups on our social studies projects today. Tell me this: What strategy helped your group make decisions together?"

. . . .

2 **Students form groups** of three to five.

. . . .

3 **Ask your first question.** Each group takes a minute or so to discuss their ideas. Then one person in each group quickly reports group members' ideas.

. . . .

4 **Repeat with your remaining questions,**
asking as many as time allows.

· · · · · · · · · · · ·

More sample questions for Step 1

➤ Today in writing we practiced capturing our readers' attention with the first sentence. Tell me this: What's one new thing you tried?

➤ Before going to the lunchroom today, we talked about different conversations you might have at your table. Tell me this: What's one topic you talked about?

125

Tricky Bear

Materials needed:

four colors of markers, enough total markers for each student to have one

Skills reinforced:

listening, keeping rhythm, reading

1 **Teach students this chant or song** (post the words; search online for the tune). Emphasize the bold syllables and give a little pause at the dashes.

*On a **Sun**–day,*
*a **Mon**–day,*
*a **Tues**day, **Wednes**day, **Thurs**day,*
*a **Fri**–day,*
*a **Satur**–day night,*

*Just be**ware***
*of the **scare***
*of the **tricky**, tricky **bear***
*on **any***
***day** or **night**.*

- - - - - - -

2 **Place a marker in front of each student.** Students chant or sing, passing the markers one at a time around the circle on the bold syllables.

- - - - - - - -

3 **Students answer a reflection question** based on the color of the marker they have at the end of the song. For example:

Blue: What's one new thing you learned today?

Red: What's one way you helped someone today?

Orange: What's something you want to try again tomorrow?

Purple: What's one way you took care of yourself today?

More sample questions for Step 3

➤ What went well for you today?

➤ On a scale of one to five, how much did you enjoy today's read-aloud?

➤ What's one thing you look forward to tomorrow?

➤ What's one way that our class followed a class rule today?

Who, What, When?

1 **Prepare cards** for *Who, What, When, Where, Why,* and *How* before the closing circle (use the reproducibles at right). Put these cards into a basket or box that can be passed around the circle.

2 **Each student in turn takes out a card** and recalls something from the day that relates to the card. For example, "I learned HOW to write a bibliography today" or "I found out WHERE Algeria is on a map."

3 **The student then returns the card** and passes the basket or box to the next person.

128

Who?	What?
Who?	Who?
When?	Where?
Why?	How?

Many people pulled together to create this book.
We are grateful to:

Susan Roser, our cheerleader, advisor, friend, and mentor throughout this entire process.

Mike Anderson, Sarah Fillion, Sue French, Lisa Garsh, Tracey Mercier, Regis Murphy, Sue Rakow, Margaret Wilson, and the many other consulting teachers with whom we have the pleasure of working. Thanks for sharing your ideas and classroom wisdom.

Elizabeth Nash for her copyediting and Helen Merena for her book design.

Alice Yang, our editor, whose positive energy, encouragement, and expertise guided us in our first writing venture.

Our workshop participants, who showed us the need for this book and shared their ideas.

The manuscript readers and child artists who contributed to this book.

I would additionally like to thank Sarah, Rachel, Meredith, Lauren, and Michele for being supportive and helping with many of the activities in this book and Kristen for sharing her evenings, weekends, and holidays. Special thanks to my family: my husband, Michael, and our girls, Mary and Madelyn, who cheer me on and are patient and supportive.

—*Dana Januszka*

. . . .

I would additionally like to thank Dana for her dedication to this project. My husband, Andrew, and our daughter, Brooke, gave me the space and time to write. Special thanks for their encouragement, understanding, and support.

—*Kristen Vincent*

. . . .

Dana Januszka and Kristen Vincent are experienced teachers with long histories of using the *Responsive Classroom* approach to teaching. They present *Responsive Classroom* workshops to educators across the country.

Dana began her teaching career as a kindergarten teacher in South Brunswick, New Jersey, and then taught kindergarten through fifth grade gifted and talented. She is currently a *Responsive Classroom* consulting teacher.

 Kristen began her teaching career as an educator at the New England Aquarium in Boston, Massachusetts, and then taught fourth grade at Newman Elementary in Needham, Massachusetts, for eight years. She is currently a *Responsive Classroom* consulting teacher.

Explore these other great resources from Center
for Responsive Schools, available from
www.responsiveclassroom.org.

80 Morning Meeting Ideas for Grades K–2
by Susan Lattanzi Roser. 2012.

80 Morning Meeting Ideas for Grades 3–6
by Carol Davis. 2012.

*Interactive Modeling: A Powerful Technique for
Teaching Children* by Margaret Berry Wilson.
2012.

*Energizers! 88 Quick Movement Activities That
Refresh and Refocus* by Susan Lattanzi Roser.
2009.

The Morning Meeting Book, 3rd ed., by Roxann
Kriete and Carol Davis. 2014.

Center for Responsive Schools, Inc., a not-for-profit educational organization, is the developer of *Responsive Classroom®*, an evidence-based education approach associated with greater teacher effectiveness, higher student achievement, and improved school climate. *Responsive Classroom* practices help educators build competencies in four interrelated domains: engaging academics, positive community, effective management, and developmentally responsive teaching. We offer the following resources for educators:

Professional Development Services

* Workshops for K–8 educators (locations around the country and internationally)
* On-site consulting services to support implementation
* Resources for site-based study
* Annual conferences for K–8 educators

Publications and Resources

* Books on a wide variety of *Responsive Classroom* topics
* Professional development kits for school-based study
* Free monthly newsletter
* Extensive library of free articles on our website

For details, contact:

Center for Responsive Schools, Inc.
85 Avenue A, P.O. Box 718, Turners Falls, Massachusetts 01376-0718
800-360-6332   www.responsiveclassroom.org
info@responsiveclassroom.org